G000069250

Improve your scales!

A workbook for examinations

Clarinet Grades 4–5

Paul Harris

Contents

See Improve your scales! *Clarinet Grades 1–3 for work pages on F, G and C majors, and G and D minors*

© 1994 by Faber Music Ltd
First published in 1994 by Faber Music Ltd
Revised impression 2002
Bloomsbury House 74–77 Great Russell Street London WC1B 3DA
Cover illustration by Drew Hillier
Printed in England by Caligraving Ltd
All rights reserved

ISBN10: 0-571-51476-6
EAN13: 978-0-571-51476-2

To buy Faber Music publications or to find out about the full range of titles available
please contact your local music retailer or Faber Music sales enquiries:

Faber Music Ltd, Burnt Mill, Elizabeth Way, Harlow CM20 2HX England
Tel: +44 (0)1279 82 89 82   Fax: +44 (0)1279 82 89 83

Introduction

To the student

Have you ever realised that it is much easier to learn something if you want to? Do you ever forget your telephone number? How many characters can you name from your favourite 'soap' or football team? Scales are not difficult to learn if you really want to learn them. Not only will they improve many aspects of your technique, but you will also get high marks in the scale section of grade exams, you will be able to learn pieces more quickly (difficult passages are often nothing more than scale patterns) and your sight-reading will improve too! Treat scales as friends – they will pay you great dividends!

To the teacher

Scales and arpeggios are often a real stumbling block for exam candidates and budding musicians. *Improve your scales!* is designed to make scale preparation and learning fun!

Working through the book will encourage your pupils to approach scales and arpeggios methodically and thoughtfully. It will help with memory problems and turn scale-learning into an enjoyable experience.

Simultaneous learning

Scales, sight-reading and aural are often the aspects of teaching relegated to the final few minutes of a lesson. The link between scales (particularly in the development of 'key-sense' and the recognition of melodic/harmonic patterns) and sight-reading is obvious, and there are many ways to integrate aural into the process too. Thus the use of the material in this book as a more central feature of a lesson is strongly recommended, especially when used in conjunction with *Improve your sight-reading!* Pupils will learn to become more musically aware, make fewer mistakes and allow the teacher to concentrate on teaching the music!

Using the book

The purpose of this workbook is to incorporate regular scale playing into lessons and daily practice and to help pupils prepare for grade examinations. You need not work at all sections, nor in the order as set out, but the best results may well be achieved by adhering fairly closely to the material.

Know the Notes! is to prove that the actual notes are known! Students should be encouraged to say the notes up and down until this can be done really fluently.

The **Finger Fitness** exercises are to strengthen the fingers and to cover technically tricky areas. They should be played legato, detached, staccato and any other form of mixed articulation that you can devise! When they are fluent you may like to add dynamic levels and vary the rhythmic patterns. Always encourage an active awareness of intonation. It is recommended that these exercises are played slowly until real control is achieved.

The **Scale Study** and **Arpeggio Study** are really extended exercises, but place the material in a more musical and 'fun' context. Some have *ad lib.* accompaniments or you might like to improvise a simple piano accompaniment; this would add interest and help the student with intonation and time.

Have a go is to encourage thought 'in the key', through the improvisation or composition of a short tune.

As a further exercise to develop the ability to think in a key, encourage pupils to play (by ear) a well known melody – for example, 'Happy Birthday' or the National Anthem (major), 'Greensleeves' or 'God rest ye merry, gentlemen' (minor). You might like to ask pupils to improvise a simple variation on their chosen melody. This could be rhythmic or dynamic to begin. As they grow in confidence they might try 'decorating' the melody.

Say→Think→Play! is where the student finally plays the scale and arpeggio. The following method should really help in memorising each scale and arpeggio:

1 **Say** the notes out loud, up and down, and repeat until fluent.
2 Say the notes out loud and finger the scale. Don't proceed further until this can be done confidently and accurately.
3 **Think** the notes and finger the scale (but don't play out loud).
4 Think the notes and **play** the scale/arpeggio. By this time there should be no doubt in the player's mind and there should certainly be no fumbles or wrong notes!

Marking

A marking system has been included to help you and the student to monitor progress and to act as a means of encouragement. It is suggested you adopt a grading system as follows:

A Excellent work!
B Good work, but keep at it!
C A little more practice would be a good idea!
D No time to lose – get practising at once!

Revision

At the end of each stage you will find a **Revision Practice** table. As the new scales become more familiar you will wish your student to revise them regularly. This table is to encourage a methodical approach to scale practice, and show that there are endless ways of practising scales and arpeggios! Fill out the table for each week, or each practice session as follows:

1 Mark **L** for legato, **D** for detached and **S** for staccato, or;

2 Choose a different articulation pattern each time from the following: Scales:

Arpeggios:

3 Choose a different rhythmic pattern each time from the following:

4 Finally, choose a different dynamic level. As students get into the habit of good scale and arpeggio practice they should no longer need the table.

Group Teaching

Improve your scales! is ideal for group teaching. Members of the group should be asked to comment on performances of the **Finger Fitness** exercises – was the tone even? Were the fingers moving rhythmically and together when necessary? Was the pulse even? *etc*. Exercises could be split between two or more players (for example, playing alternate phrases), and constructive criticism should be encouraged for the scale and arpeggio studies. With the optional *ad lib.* parts, a small group of the pieces could be performed at a private 'group concert', or even at a more formal concert.

Bb major 2 octaves (see *Improve your scales!* Clarinet Grades 1–3 for more practice material)

Know the Notes!

1 Write the key signature of Bb major:

2 Write out the notes of the scale:

Bb	C	D	Eb	F	G	A	Bb

3 Write out the notes of the arpeggio:

Bb	D	F	Bb

Finger Fitness

Always practice the **Finger Fitness** exercises legato, detached and staccato (see Introduction).

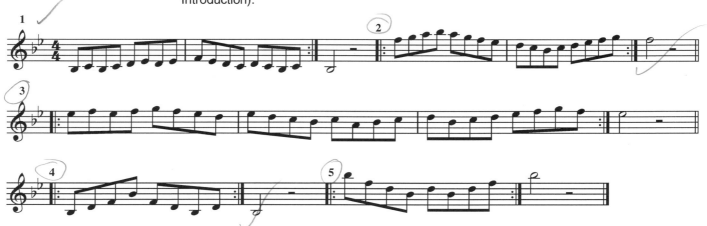

Bilberry Blossom

Scale study in Bb major

Bleak Blizzard Blues

Arpeggio study in B♭ major

Have a go

Compose or improvise your own tune in B♭ major. If you are writing your tune down, remember to put in some markings and then give your piece a title.

Say

Think

Play!

Say the notes out loud, up and down, then say the notes out loud and finger the scale/arpeggio.

Think the notes and finger the scale/arpeggio.

Play the scale and arpeggio.

Revision Practice

B♭ major (2 octaves)	1	2	3	4	5	6	7	8	9	10
Legato/Detached/Staccato										
Articulation pattern										
Rhythmic pattern										
Dynamic level										

Marking

B♭ major (2 octaves)	Grade
Know the notes!	
Finger fitness	
Scale study	
Arpeggio study	
Have a go	
Say → think → play!	

A major 2 octaves

(see *Improve your scales!* Clarinet Grades 1–3 for more practice material)

Know the Notes!

1 Write the key signature of A major:

2 Write out the notes of the scale: A B C# D E F# G# A

3 Write out the notes of the arpeggio: A C# E A

Finger Fitness

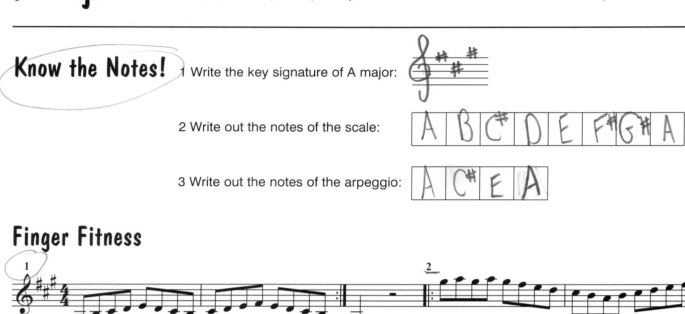

Alien Allegro

Scale study in A major

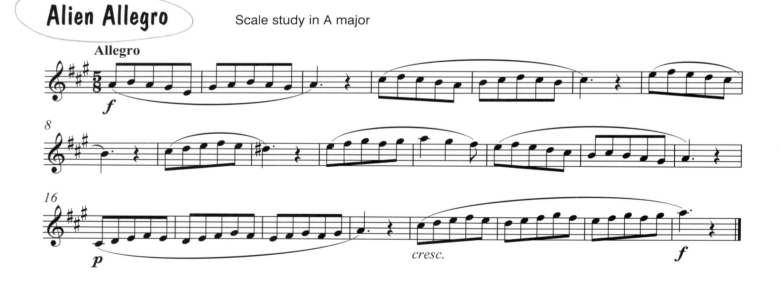

7th June

Amusement Arcade Arpeggio study in A major

* Player 2 may start at the beginning when Player 1 reaches this point (optional)

Have a go Compose or improvise your own tune in A major

Say

Say the notes out loud, up and down, then say the notes out loud and finger the scale/arpeggio.

Think

Think the notes and finger the scale/arpeggio.

Play!

Play the scale and arpeggio.

Revision Practice

A major (2 octaves)	1	2	3	4	5	6	7	8	9	10
Legato/Detached/Staccato										
Articulation pattern										
Rhythmic pattern										
Dynamic level										

Marking

A major (2 octaves)	Grade
Know the notes!	
Finger fitness	
Scale study	
Arpeggio study	
Have a go	
Say → think → play!	

D major 2 octaves (see *Improve your scales!* Clarinet Grades 1–3 for more practice material)

Know the Notes!

1 Write the key signature of D major:

2 Write out the notes of the scale:

| D | E | F# | G | A | B | C# | D |

3 Write out the notes of the arpeggio:

| D | F# | A | D |

Finger Fitness

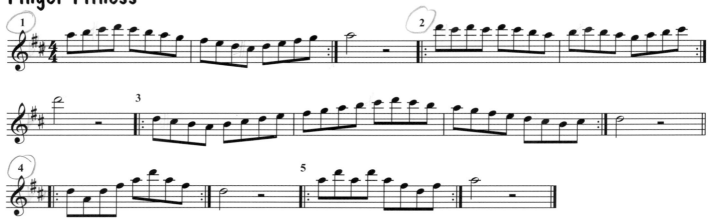

Dastardly Dance   Scale study in D major

Dozey Dog

Arpeggio study in D major

Have a go

Compose or improvise your own tune in D major

Say

Think

Play!

Say the notes out loud, up and down, then say the notes out loud and finger the scale/arpeggio.

Think the notes and finger the scale/arpeggio.

Play the scale and arpeggio.

Revision Practice

D major (2 octaves)	1	2	3	4	5	6	7	8	9	10
Legato/Detached/Staccato										
Articulation pattern										
Rhythmic pattern										
Dynamic level										

Marking

D major (2 octaves)	Grade
Know the notes!	
Finger fitness	
Scale study	
Arpeggio study	
Have a go	
Say → think → play!	

E harmonic minor 2 octaves

Know the Notes!

1 Write the key signature of E minor:

2 Write out the notes of the scale:

E	F#G	A	B	C	d#e

3 Write out the notes of the arpeggio:

E	G	B	E

Finger Fitness

Eccentric Elephant

Scale study in E harmonic minor

Escalator

Arpeggio study in E minor

Have a go

Compose or improvise your own tune using the notes of E harmonic minor.

Say

Think

Play!

Say the notes out loud, up and down, then say the notes out loud and finger the scale/arpeggio.

Think the notes and finger the scale/arpeggio.

Play the scale and arpeggio.

Revision Practice

E harmonic minor (2 octaves)	1	2	3	4	5	6	7	8	9	10
Legato/Detached/Staccato										
Articulation pattern										
Rhythmic pattern										
Dynamic level										

Marking

E harmonic minor (2 octaves)	Grade
Know the notes!	
Finger fitness	
Scale study	
Arpeggio study	
Have a go	
Say → think → play!	

E melodic minor 2 octaves

Know the Notes!

1 Write the key signature of E minor:

2 Write out the notes of the scale:

up→						
						←down

3 Write out the notes of the arpeggio:

Finger Fitness

Elizabethan Elegy

Scale study in E melodic minor

Elegant Eclair

Arpeggio study in E minor

Have a go

Compose or improvise your own tune using the notes of E melodic minor.

Say

Think

Play!

Say the notes out loud, up and down, then say the notes out loud and finger the scale/arpeggio.

Think the notes and finger the scale/arpeggio.

Play the scale and arpeggio.

Revision Practice

E melodic minor (2 octaves)	1	2	3	4	5	6	7	8	9	10
Legato/Detached/Staccato										
Articulation pattern										
Rhythmic pattern										
Dynamic level										

Marking

E melodic minor (2 octaves)	Grade
Know the notes!	
Finger fitness	
Scale study	
Arpeggio study	
Have a go	
Say → think → play!	

B harmonic minor 2 octaves

Know the Notes!

1 Write the key signature of B minor:

2 Write out the notes of the scale:

3 Write out the notes of the arpeggio:

Finger Fitness

Busy Bourée

Scale study in B harmonic minor

Brazilian Ballet   Arpeggio study in B minor

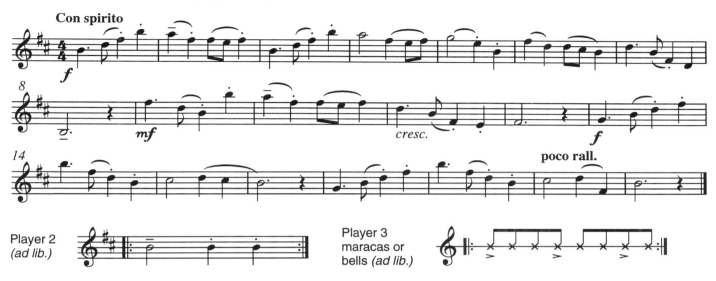

Have a go

Compose or improvise your own tune using the notes of B harmonic minor.

Say

Think

Play!

Say the notes out loud, up and down, then say the notes out loud and finger the scale/arpeggio.

Think the notes and finger the scale/arpeggio.

Play the scale and arpeggio.

Revision Practice

B harmonic minor (2 octaves)	1	2	3	4	5	6	7	8	9	10
Legato/Detached/Staccato										
Articulation pattern										
Rhythmic pattern										
Dynamic level										

Marking

B harmonic minor (2 octaves)	Grade
Know the notes!	
Finger fitness	
Scale study	
Arpeggio study	
Have a go	
Say → think → play!	

B melodic minor 2 octaves

Know the Notes!

1 Write the key signature of B minor:

2 Write out the notes of the scale:

up→						
						←down

3 Write out the notes of the arpeggio:

Finger Fitness

Burly Buccaneer Scale study in B melodic minor

Boomerang

Arpeggio study in B minor

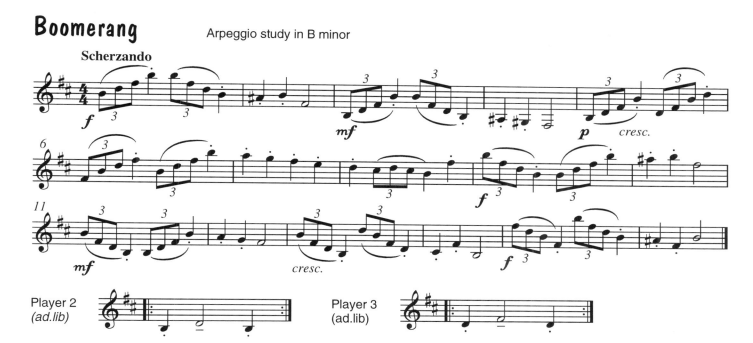

Player 2
(ad.lib)

Player 3
(ad.lib)

Have a go

Compose or improvise your own tune using the notes of B melodic minor.

Say

Think

Play!

Say the notes out loud, up and down, then say the notes out loud and finger the scale/arpeggio.

Think the notes and finger the scale/arpeggio.

Play the scale and arpeggio.

Revision Practice

B melodic minor (2 octaves)	1	2	3	4	5	6	7	8	9	10
Legato/Detached/Staccato										
Articulation pattern										
Rhythmic pattern										
Dynamic level										

Marking

B melodic minor (2 octaves)	Grade
Know the notes!	
Finger fitness	
Scale study	
Arpeggio study	
Have a go	
Say → think → play!	

C harmonic minor 2 octaves

Know the Notes!

1 Write the key signature of C minor:

2 Write out the notes of the scale:

3 Write out the notes of the arpeggio:

Finger Fitness

Carriage Clock

Scale study in C harmonic minor

Caramel Caprice
Arpeggio study in C minor

Have a go

Compose or improvise your own tune using the notes of C harmonic minor.

Say

Think

Play!

Say the notes out loud, up and down, then say the notes out loud and finger the scale/arpeggio.

Think the notes and finger the scale/arpeggio.

Play the scale and arpeggio.

Revision Practice

C harmonic minor (2 octaves)	1	2	3	4	5	6	7	8	9	10
Legato/Detached/Staccato										
Articulation pattern										
Rhythmic pattern										
Dynamic level										

Marking

C harmonic minor (2 octaves)	Grade
Know the notes!	
Finger fitness	
Scale study	
Arpeggio study	
Have a go	
Say → think → play!	

C melodic minor 2 octaves

Know the Notes!

1 Write the key signature of C minor:

2 Write out the notes of the scale:

up→						
						←down

3 Write out the notes of the arpeggio:

Finger Fitness

Chariots

Scale study in C melodic minor

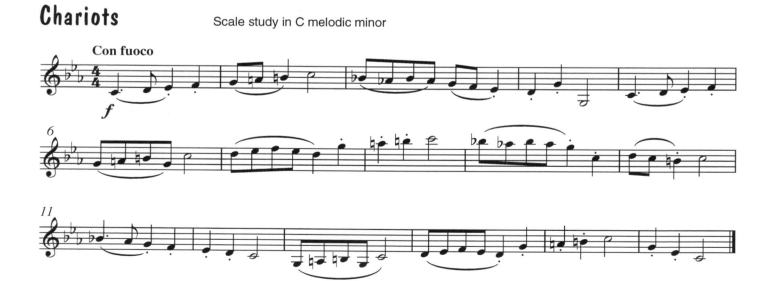

Cream Cake

Arpeggio study in C minor

Have a go

Compose or improvise your own tune using the notes of C melodic minor.

Say
Think
Play!

Say the notes out loud, up and down, then say the notes out loud and finger the scale/arpeggio.

Think the notes and finger the scale/arpeggio.

Play the scale and arpeggio.

Revision Practice

C melodic minor (2 octaves)	1	2	3	4	5	6	7	8	9	10
Legato/Detached/Staccato										
Articulation pattern										
Rhythmic pattern										
Dynamic level										

Marking

C melodic minor (2 octaves)	Grade
Know the notes!	
Finger fitness	
Scale study	
Arpeggio study	
Have a go	
Say → think → play!	

E major 2 octaves

Know the Notes!

1 Write the key signature of E major:

2 Write out the notes of the scale:

3 Write out the notes of the arpeggio:

Finger Fitness

Energetic Earwig Scale study in E major

Eerie Eel

Arpeggio study in E major

Have a go

Compose or improvise your own tune in E major.

Say

Say the notes out loud, up and down, then say the notes out loud and finger the scale/arpeggio.

Think

Think the notes and finger the scale/arpeggio.

Play!

Play the scale and arpeggio.

Revision Practice

E major (2 octaves)	1	2	3	4	5	6	7	8	9	10
Legato/Detached/Staccato										
Articulation pattern										
Rhythmic pattern										
Dynamic level										

Marking

E major (2 octaves)	Grade
Know the notes!	
Finger fitness	
Scale study	
Arpeggio study	
Have a go	
Say → think → play!	

Ab major 2 octaves

Know the Notes!

1 Write the key signature of Ab major:

2 Write out the notes of the scale:

3 Write out the notes of the arpeggio:

Finger Fitness

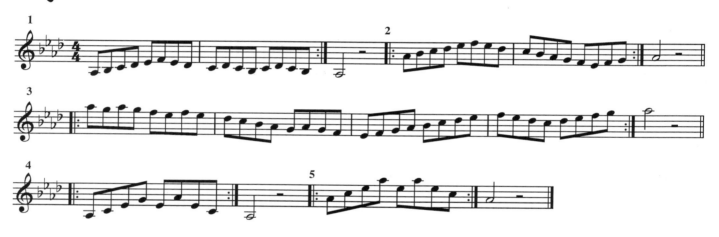

Athletic Adventure

Scale study in Ab major

Amorous Arpeggios

Arpeggio study in A♭ major

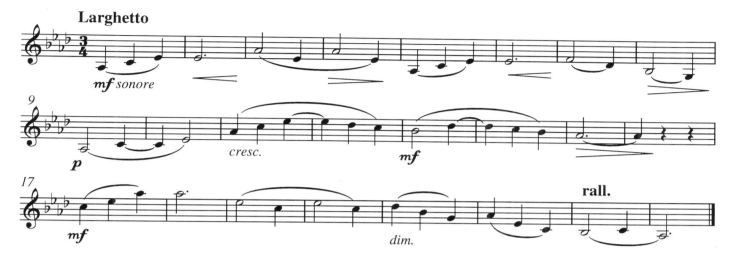

Have a go

Compose or improvise your own tune in A♭ major.

Say
Think
Play!

Say the notes out loud, up and down, then say the notes out loud and finger the scale/arpeggio.

Think the notes and finger the scale/arpeggio.

Play the scale and arpeggio.

Revision Practice

A♭ major (2 octaves)	1	2	3	4	5	6	7	8	9	10
Legato/Detached/Staccato										
Articulation pattern										
Rhythmic pattern										
Dynamic level										

Marking

A♭ major (2 octaves)	Grade
Know the notes!	
Finger fitness	
Scale study	
Arpeggio study	
Have a go	
Say → think → play!	

E♭ major 2 octaves

Know the Notes!

1 Write the key signature of E♭ major:

2 Write out the notes of the scale:

3 Write out the notes of the arpeggio:

Finger Fitness

Ebony

Scale study in E♭ major

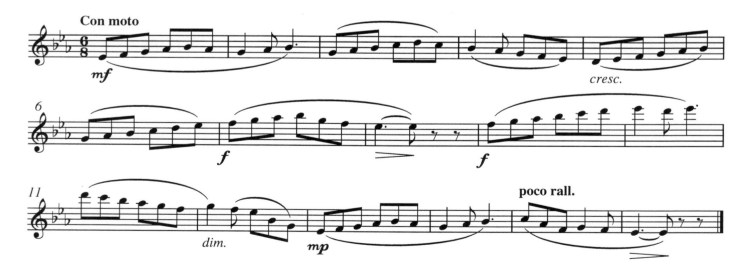

Elf

Arpeggio study in E♭ major

Player 2
(ad lib.)

Have a go

Compose or improvise your own tune in E♭ major.

Say

Say the notes out loud, up and down, then say the notes out loud and finger the scale/arpeggio.

Think

Think the notes and finger the scale/arpeggio.

Play!

Play the scale and arpeggio.

Revision Practice

E♭ major (2 octaves)	1	2	3	4	5	6	7	8	9	10
Legato/Detached/Staccato										
Articulation pattern										
Rhythmic pattern										
Dynamic level										

Marking

E♭ major (2 octaves)	Grade
Know the notes!	
Finger fitness	
Scale study	
Arpeggio study	
Have a go	
Say → think → play!	

F harmonic minor 2 octaves

Know the Notes!

1 Write the key signature of F minor:

2 Write out the notes of the scale:

3 Write out the notes of the arpeggio:

Finger Fitness

Fast Food

Scale study in F harmonic minor

Funny Fellow

Arpeggio study in F minor

Have a go

Compose or improvise your own tune using the notes of F harmonic minor.

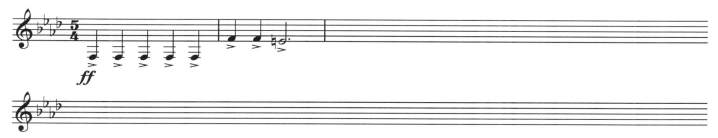

Say
Think
Play!

Say the notes out loud, up and down, then say the notes out loud and finger the scale/arpeggio.

Think the notes and finger the scale/arpeggio.

Play the scale and arpeggio.

Revision Practice

F harmonic minor (2 octaves)	1	2	3	4	5	6	7	8	9	10
Legato/Detached/Staccato										
Articulation pattern										
Rhythmic pattern										
Dynamic level										

Marking

F harmonic minor (2 octaves)	Grade
Know the notes!	
Finger fitness	
Scale study	
Arpeggio study	
Have a go	
Say → think → play!	

F melodic minor 2 octaves

Know the Notes!

1 Write the key signature of F minor:

2 Write out the notes of the scale:

up→						
						←down

3 Write out the notes of the arpeggio:

Finger Fitness

Forgotten Fancy Scale study in F melodic minor

Fantastic Finale
Arpeggio study in F minor

Have a go

Compose or improvise your own tune using the notes of F melodic minor.

Say
Think
Play!

Say the notes out loud, up and down, then say the notes out loud and finger the scale/arpeggio.

Think the notes and finger the scale/arpeggio.

Play the scale and arpeggio.

Revision Practice

F melodic minor (2 octaves)	1	2	3	4	5	6	7	8	9	10
Legato/Detached/Staccato										
Articulation pattern										
Rhythmic pattern										
Dynamic level										

Marking

F melodic minor (2 octaves)	Grade
Know the notes!	
Finger fitness	
Scale study	
Arpeggio study	
Have a go	
Say → think → play!	

F# harmonic minor 2 octaves

Know the Notes!

1 Write the key signature of F# minor:

2 Write out the notes of the scale:

3 Write out the notes of the arpeggio:

Finger Fitness

Frisky Fingers

Scale study in F# harmonic minor

Friendly Ferret

Arpeggio study in F# minor

Have a go

Compose or improvise your own tune using the notes of F# harmonic minor.

Say
Think
Play!

Say the notes out loud, up and down, then say the notes out loud and finger the scale/arpeggio.

Think the notes and finger the scale/arpeggio.

Play the scale and arpeggio.

Revision Practice

F# harmonic minor (2 octaves)	1	2	3	4	5	6	7	8	9	10
Legato/Detached/Staccato										
Articulation pattern										
Rhythmic pattern										
Dynamic level										

Marking

F# harmonic minor (2 octaves)	Grade
Know the notes!	
Finger fitness	
Scale study	
Arpeggio study	
Have a go	
Say → think → play!	

F♯ melodic minor 2 octaves

Know the Notes!

1 Write the key signature of F♯ minor:

2 Write out the notes of the scale:

up→						
						←down

3 Write out the notes of the arpeggio:

Finger Fitness

Fabulous Fable

Scale study in F♯ melodic minor

Fives Fantasy

Arpeggio study in F# minor

Have a go

Compose or improvise your own tune using the notes of F# melodic minor.

Say

Think

Play!

Say the notes out loud, up and down, then say the notes out loud and finger the scale/arpeggio.

Think the notes and finger the scale/arpeggio.

Play the scale and arpeggio.

Revision Practice

F# melodic minor (2 octaves)	1	2	3	4	5	6	7	8	9	10
Legato/Detached/Staccato										
Articulation pattern										
Rhythmic pattern										
Dynamic level										

Marking

F# melodic minor (2 octaves)	Grade
Know the notes!	
Finger fitness	
Scale study	
Arpeggio study	
Have a go	
Say → think → play!	

C♯ harmonic minor 2 octaves

Know the Notes!

1 Write the key signature of C♯ minor:

2 Write out the notes of the scale:

3 Write out the notes of the arpeggio:

Finger Fitness

Comedy Carnival in Cairo

Scale study in C♯ harmonic minor

Clarissa

Arpeggio study in C♯ minor

*Use top line if only one extra player is available

*Player 2 *(ad lib.)*
Player 3 *(ad lib.)*

Have a go

Compose or improvise your own tune using the notes of C♯ harmonic minor.

Say
Think
Play!

Say the notes out loud, up and down, then say the notes out loud and finger the scale/arpeggio.

Think the notes and finger the scale/arpeggio.

Play the scale and arpeggio.

Revision Practice

C♯ harmonic minor (2 octaves)	1	2	3	4	5	6	7	8	9	10
Legato/Detached/Staccato										
Articulation pattern										
Rhythmic pattern										
Dynamic level										

Marking

C♯ harmonic minor (2 octaves)	Grade
Know the notes!	
Finger fitness	
Scale study	
Arpeggio study	
Have a go	
Say → think → play!	

C# melodic minor 2 octaves

Know the Notes!

1 Write the key signature of C# minor:

2 Write out the notes of the scale:

3 Write out the notes of the arpeggio:

Finger Fitness

Cheese 'n' Chilli Scale study in C# melodic minor

Circles

Arpeggio study in C♯ minor

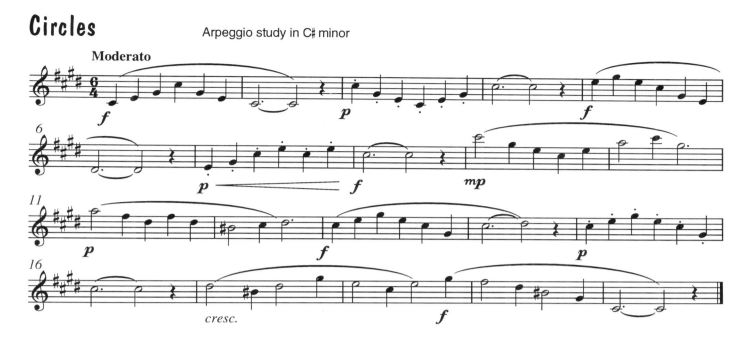

Have a go

Compose or improvise your own tune using the notes of C♯ melodic minor.

Say
Think
Play!

Say the notes out loud, up and down, then say the notes out loud and finger the scale/arpeggio.

Think the notes and finger the scale/arpeggio.

Play the scale and arpeggio.

Revision Practice

C♯ melodic minor (2 octaves)	1	2	3	4	5	6	7	8	9	10
Legato/Detached/Staccato										
Articulation pattern										
Rhythmic pattern										
Dynamic level										

Marking

C♯ melodic minor (2 octaves)	Grade
Know the notes!	
Finger fitness	
Scale study	
Arpeggio study	
Have a go	
Say → think → play!	

Performance tips

1. Always play scales and arpeggios with your best tone quality.

2. Tone quality must be as even as possible throughout.

3. Don't land on the last note with a 'bump'.

4. Finger movement should always be firm and precise.

5. Rhythm must be even, and pulse steady throughout.

6. Make sure all notes are of equal duration in tongued scales and arpeggios.

7. Don't change tempo or lose rhythmic control when you change direction.

8. Don't accent the top note.

9. Always play scales carefully in tune.

10. Make sure that your finger movement is well co-ordinated in arpeggios.

11. At exams, play all scales at the same tempo and about *mezzo-forte* (*mf*).

12. Remember that scales *are* music; play each one with shape and direction.

Scales and arpeggios

SCALES AND ARPEGGIOS (exam requirements of the Associated Board)
From memory, to be played both slurred and tongued in the indicated keys for each Grade:

GRADE 4: F, G, A, B♭, D majors; E, G, B, C, D minors* (two octaves)
Chromatic Scales: starting on F and C (two octaves)
Dominant Seventh: in the key of C (two octaves)

GRADE 5: E, G, A♭, B♭, C, D, E♭ majors; F, F♯, B, C, C♯, D minors* (two octaves)
Chromatic Scales: starting on F and C (two octaves)
Dominant Sevenths: in the keys of B♭, C and D (two octaves)
Diminished Seventh: starting on G (two octaves)

*Scales: in the above keys (minors in melodic *or* harmonic form at candidate's choice)
Arpeggios: the common chords of the above keys for the range indicated.

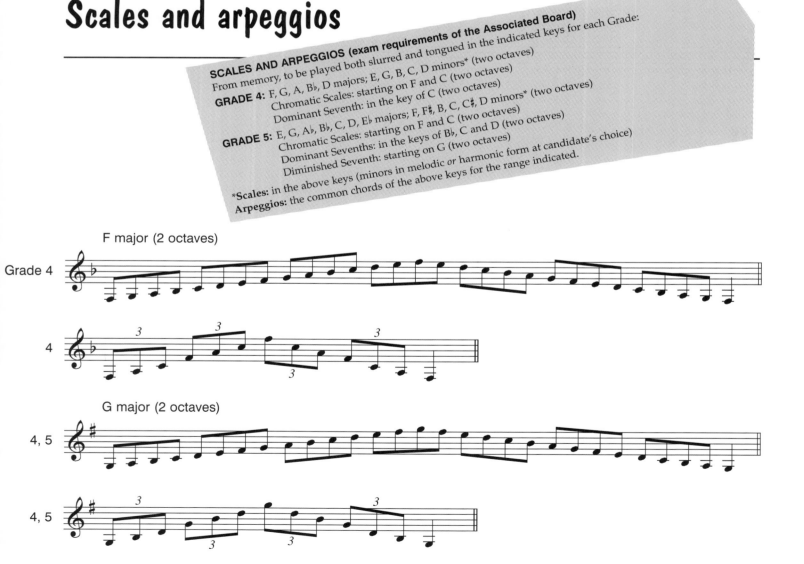

41

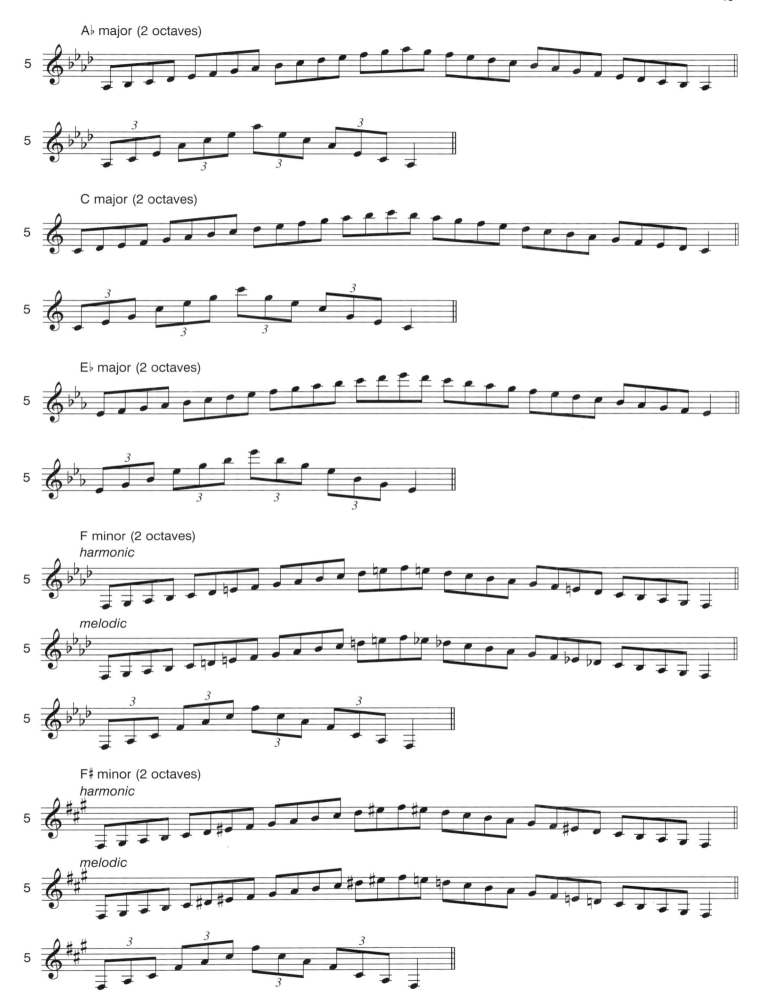

44

C# minor (2 octaves)
harmonic

melodic

Chromatic scale on F (2 octaves)

Chromatic scale on C (2 octaves)

Dominant 7th in C (2 octaves)

Dominant 7th in B♭ (2 octaves)

Dominant 7th in D (2 octaves)

Diminished 7th on G (2 octaves)

Welcome to …

Paul Harris's
Clarinet Basics

A method for individual
and group learning

Clarinet Basics is a landmark method by one of the leading figures in clarinet education. It starts at absolute beginner level and progresses to about Grade 2 level. The method is set out in 22 stages, each of which includes:

- a wonderful variety of concert pieces from the great composers

- traditional tunes and fun, original exercises

- 'finger gyms' and 'warm ups' to help establish a sound technique

- invaluable 'fact files' and 'quizzes' to teach notation and general musicianship

- helpful, clear 'fingering charts' and 'rhythm boxes'

- great illustrations!

The separate teacher's book contains clarinet and piano accompaniments, suggestions for group work and teaching tips.

Clarinet Basics (pupil's book) ISBN 0-571-51814-1
Clarinet Basics (teacher's book) ISBN 0-571-51815-X

Also available:
Andy Hampton's Saxophone Basics
Pupil's book ISBN 0-571-51972-5 Teacher's book ISBN 0-571-51973-3

UNBEATEN TRACKS

8 contemporary pieces for Clarinet and Piano

Edited by Paul Harris

ISBN 0-571-52003-0

Unbeaten Tracks is a ground-breaking new series of specially commissioned pieces for the intermediate player. Combining works by established and up-and-coming composers, this volume brings contemporary music within the reach of the less experienced clarinettist. The eight pieces (of roughly grade 4 to 7 standard) are written in an array of musical styles, and are an exciting adventure into fresh musical sound worlds.

Christopher Gunning	*Reluctant Ragtime*
Richard Harris	*Escapology*
John Hawkins	*Night Run*
Eddie McGuire	*Elegiac Waltz*
Lloyd Moore	*Lower Ground*
Edward Rushton	*Clay*
Peter Sculthorpe	*Reef Singing*
Huw Watkins	*March*

FABER *ff* MUSIC

Clarinet volumes from Faber Music

FABER MUSIC · 3 QUEEN SQUARE · LONDON
www.fabermusic.com

Are you paralysed with fear
every time you go on stage?

Discover how to turn nerves
to your advantage.

CONFIDENCE-BOOSTING STRATEGIES
for musicians and performers

KEEPING
YOUR
NERVE!

Kate Jones

FABER *ff* MUSIC

3. If you are not a pianist, try and make sure you have as much practice with your accompanist as possible. It's important that you know the accompaniment as well. After all, it is part of the music! And don't be afraid of your accompanist. You are the soloist and they are there to make music with you. The same goes for ensemble playing. Getting to know your colleagues and how they may deal with nerves is as important as practising the notes.

Don't be afraid of your accompanist ...

4. If you are playing several pieces in your recital and you are able to devise the programme order, it is often helpful to start with a piece you know well or a piece that isn't too technically demanding. This way you allow yourself the best warming-up conditions and are more likely to control your nerves.

5. Make sure you like the music you are playing. Enjoying what you do is another key element to reducing any nerves you may feel. It's your performance and you need to be in control.

12

8. Allow ... predict what ... a contingency plan so that if you ... ust sitting around. See if there is a park or a café nearby where you could use any spare time you have doing something not connected with the impending performance. Above all, use the time to relax.

Allow plenty of time to get to the venue, as you can never predict what might happen en route ...

13

Keeping your nerve! is the perfect prop for the young or amateur performer affected by stage fright. Full of comforting, easy-to-find advice and amusing anecdotes, this book will help you to:

· prepare for your performance, whether for a concert or exam
· enjoy performing, wherever and whenever
· unwind after the performance
· understand why you perform and why your audience turns up

Kate Jones also teams up with a star-studded cast of sympathetic performers and teachers, including Joanna MacGregor, Elvis Costello and Steven Isserlis, who reveal the special tactics that prevent them from turning to jelly!

"An invaluable, wonderful book. This must be in every musician's hands, young or old!"
(*Evelyn Glennie*)

Keeping your nerve!   ISBN 0-571-51922-9